# TRIED AND TRUE GRADUATION TIPS

## What We Know For Sure About Graduation and Beyond

by Terry Matthews-Lombardo, CMP

ISBN: 1508426910
ISBN-13: 978-1508426912

.

# DEDICATION

To all graduates, you have not finished learning!  Realize
that the life before you is one giant open book, so keep
reading.

# CONTENTS

# PREFACE

What we know for sure is that there is no one definitive manual for life training, so this book is meant to be a short, sweet, and sensible guide to genuine things a graduate needs to know before going out in the real world.

Now, I'm sure all the graduates reading this probably think they already know more than their parents, right? And as parents, we know for sure that we know more than our kids, right? Well for now, let's use this book as a meeting of the minds and agree to agree while we take a brief eye opening journey into the world in which we all cohabitate and travel with each other.

First, let's talk about the actual graduation itself. You know the event where grads regally march down the aisle while Pomp and Circumstance is majestically playing in the background. The fact of the matter is that graduation involves a whole lot of things. Studying. Testing. Praying. Dreaming. Emotions, both high and low. Preparations. Anxiety. Paperwork. Communication. The list is endless, and the more excited and organized you are the earlier the planning begins for this sacred day. As a grad, you are hit earlier than you can ever imagine. One day you're a carefree freshman student carrying what you perceive to be the weight of the world's problems in your backpack as you walk around campus trying to find your way. And in the blink of an eye you are seemingly thrown into the thick of things at your own graduation party, wondering, perhaps even fearful, of what lies ahead.

As parents, you start with the mindset of "This is going to be the best graduation ever! I'm going to relive my own big day and make our precious (insert name of son/daughter) the best event possible. They've earned this celebration and we all deserve to party!"

As kids, at this point you may just be thinking you want to crawl back into the comfort of the womb.

Mothers, fathers, sons, daughters, other siblings, grandparents and relatives – everyone gets involved, or should we say 'invited to the festivities'. This is true even if you aren't having any official celebrations. You see, the truth of the matter is that graduation is not just for the graduate. It's for everyone who even thinks they played a part in getting junior to the point of donning the cap and gown.

In some families, this is truly a once in a lifetime milestone and by all means should be celebrated to the nth degree. But for others, graduation (whether high school or college) is expected, and further, it's not so much an event as it is a passage. High school diploma? Check. College degree? Check-check. Job to follow? (Pause). (Sigh). (?). No job? More schooling? Another degree? Grad or law school? So many decisions and it seems they are all hitting at once, but graduates should remember you do have the rest of your life to figure things out. What's that, you parents say? No, you want them off your payroll now, and you fully intend to turn their now-vacant bedroom into that fitness center/office/craft room/storage closet you've always wanted as soon as possible? Well yes, we realize that's always the goal. But in the new world order, let's face it, the reality is this: (some) kids are staying home longer. Many times at the encouragement of the same parents who, just last week, wanted them out the door. Some are taking more time to research the world (aka finding an internship, and then another, followed by yet another. . .) before they commit to what they think might be a lifelong career. Some are lacking motivation. Some fear walking out the front door on their own. Some can't make a decision. Period.

Parents, we don't mean to scare you with these realities, especially so early in this book. Despite what you may be thinking right now, we do want you to continue reading until the end. Our sincere hope is that the information contained herein will be helpful, even useful to the point that it will assist both you and your graduate to prepare for what lies ahead. You see, no matter when they leave the womb, at some point in their lives your kids will move on. This we know for sure. Why not prepare and work together to make this transition a more efficient and gentle one for all?

It's a known fact that the world is scary enough once you're out there on your own, so now that we're all adults, let's try to face the inevitable together, and armed with the best possible toolkit to follow the ever popular Nike mantra of "let's do it!"

So graduates of any level – young, old, smart, challenged, scared, assured, – congratulations for making it to what you think is the end of your book learning! What we know now for sure is that you have only just begun. Your first lesson post-graduation is to realize that the life before you is one giant open book, so keep reading!

**"In all things, success depends upon previous preparation, and without such preparation there is sure to be failure." (Confucius, and/or your parents)**

# 1

# GROUND RULES IN LIFE
# THAT NEVER FAIL

Grads, we know you're already thinking "I HATE rules! I want to go out in the world where FREEDOM ROCKS!" Well guess what? Even in our 'free' society there are still plenty of rules. You already know a whole bunch of them like eat your daily fruits and veggies, don't pick your nose in public, change your underwear every day (please), don't park where it says (duh) 'don't park here'. For purposes of this discussion, we technically don't even consider those examples as rules because they fall more under the category of common sense guidelines that we naturally adhere to in a civilized society. One would assume you learned them early on from your parents, at the same time they were teaching you that whole business about right from wrong. Agreed?

The rules we want to review with you now are slightly more complex. These are things that, if your institution of higher learning did not include them in their curriculum (and we suspect they didn't), you need to pay close attention to now. Especially if you want to succeed in the class you are immediately enrolled in after graduation, also known as Life Management and/or Reality. We know that in most cases you did not officially register for this class, but just as sure as your body now wants to sleep in until noon each and every day, it's a given that the day after graduation you are now officially enrolled in LM101. Further, the bad news is that there's still a fee because as you already know, nothing is free, right? So, let's just accept the inevitable and move on with the rules that some might refer to simply as tips for navigating what lies ahead.

RULE #1 – LEARN TO MANAGE YOUR MONEY. Depending on how you were raised, this may or may not come easily to you. Rest assured, if you accept it as a rule to live by you will go far in life.

RULE#2 – LIVE WITHIN A BUDGET. Yes, we realize this should be a given if you adhere to rule #1, but let's face it, we all fall off the wagon now and again and it's critical that you get this whole money thing straight in your head early in the game. It makes moving forward so much better.

RULE #3 – BE OPEN AND ACCEPTING OF MORE LEARNING AHEAD. After graduation we're certain you might be at the point where you firmly believe you never want to crack open another textbook again in your life. However, the learning we're referring to here does not involve formal classrooms. No matter what the name and title on your degree, this learning opportunity could also be called humbling yourself. Contrary to what is written about this being a free society, learning more often than not comes at a price. For instance, you normally would only need to forget to put oil in the car once in your life because when the engine burns out and has to be replaced you will quickly realize how expensive that lesson in life management was and never repeat it again. Don't plan on owning a car anytime soon? Try joining a 'no fee involved' health club or applying for a 'free' credit card and you will learn the same expensive principal as the person who forgets to put oil in the car.

Enough said? Accept that your ongoing continuing education about life will take place in many different sizes, shapes and forms, and to that end, don't limit yourself to the 'I'm on a need to know' basis. Once you've landed a job, be open to joining a special task force committee at work or signing up for something different at the YMCA like Tai Chi classes. These are all opportunities for mind expansion, and unlike those times in school when you thought your head was going to explode if you had to cram for another useless-to-me-now chemistry exam, they can open up other worlds that you never knew existed.

RULE #4 – UNDERSTAND THAT COMMUNICATION IS PARAMOUNT TO SURVIVAL. Even if you fancy yourself as a loner, there is a basic level of interaction required to complete each and every day. Only animals in the wild get by with non-verbal communication; human interaction involves various skill levels in all of the following: talking, reading, writing, comprehending, listening, and even the management of body language. Yes, it is possible to rob a bank with only a threatening look and the show of a gun, but that still qualifies as communication. The quicker you understand that people with strong communication skills dominate the planet more keys to the universe will unfold for you.

RULE #5 – ASK QUESTIONS. This is actually a support theme to all of the above, but we can't stress it enough. It's how you learn, understand, and manage the gigantic daily flow of information that crowds our lives. Even if you were an introvert with a capital I prior to this point in your life, in order to live a successfully independent existence you must grasp the importance of asking questions and seeking advice. Now, we know many of you are thinking that's what Google is for, right? Well, remember when you were frantically writing that theme paper the night before it was due and your computer crashed? Or, the project was done but the printer didn't work?  You learned then that systems will fail, internet connections can go down, and as you may have also already discovered, mom and dad aren't always available to bail you out.  An additional side benefit in practicing this rule is that you will learn it is equally important to whom you choose to address your questions.  We hate to point out the obvious, but if your older sibling has already filed for bankruptcy at age 30 you most likely would not seek them out for financial advice, right?  (There, that was question asking already in action!)

Okay, you might be thinking there should be tons more rules to cover, and you're right.  But we promised short and simple guidelines here and must keep our promise.  (Although, now that we think about it, the principle itself of keeping things short and sweet could be viewed as another important road rule in life.  But since you're fresh off the track of listening to endless hours of lectures from boring, self-involved professors who constantly speak in seminar hoping beyond hope that their students were really listening and/or cared about the philosophy behind 'the macro environment analysis of economic frameworks in corporate America' [?], we're thinking you already realize the wisdom in the 'KISS' rule.  Enough said)

So parents, how about considering an open discussion on all of the above prior to your graduate moving out/away/back home?  If you're brave and smart enough to do this, please see the Bonus Reading at the conclusion of this book for a sample of what this author composed and gave to her own kids upon their graduations.

And finally grads, please pay particular attention to Rule #5 above when you're around your parents and mentors.  Assuming they are sage and wise people (ahem), whatever questions you ask will be music to their ears.  They will hear, "Yes!  My kid still needs me and thinks I have some answers!"  Another benefit of asking questions of those closest to you will be that this also acts as preparation to your transition of being forced to have conversations with real adult people who are already functioning in the world as opposed to the students you've been surrounded with that are only concerned with things like where this weekend's party will be held as well as drinking/texting/Face booking and finishing school to get out in the world. Think job interviews, moving out on your own and meeting the landlord and neighbors, etc. Try as you might to avoid conversations, if you want to leave home and be out on your own, mastering this skill alone will come in handy.

**"The difference between failure and success is doing a thing nearly right and doing it exactly right." [Edward C. Simmons]**

2

# YOUR MOTHER WASN'T
# KIDDING ABOUT
# THOSE MANNERS

No joke.  Good manners will take you far.  Does that sound familiar?   It should, because we're certain your parents have repeated that many times.  Someone, perhaps your grandmother or a well-meaning aunt, also might have given you a copy of some gigantic book of manners and etiquette for your graduation present.  If so, we're betting that when you opened it (ahem) your first thoughts – well, first thoughts after you came to grips with the fact that it wasn't a cash gift – were "Who would ever read this whole thing?" and "Why on earth are manners so important that they could occupy this much paper?" These were quickly followed by thoughts like "Etiquette-schmetiquette!  What the heck is that?" and, "Why oh why don't people realize kids my age don't read these things???" So, in an effort to save you time (and, if we can get to your grandmother before she buys the book, save her money), in this short chapter we are going to summarize what you need to know about manners, etiquette and civility as they pertain to moving forward in life.  Here it is, and please feel free to take notes:

MANNERS ARE REALLY, REALLY IMPORTANT.

ETIQUETTE IS JUST ANOTHER TERM FOR DOING THE RIGHT THING, aka MANNERS. (Actually, it's a French term loosely translated that means 'name tag', which in essence, is a throwback to times when it was proper to wear some identification so that instead of saying 'hey you' which we all regard as bad manners, oui?, people would know what your name was. Comprenez?)

CIVILITY IS WHAT KEEPS OUR SOCIETY IN CHECK. WITHOUT IT WE WOULD MOST LIKELY ALL BE (fill in the blank of worst case scenarios of humanity, or the lack thereof).

There now, aren't you glad we saved you all that time it would take to read the 1200+ page manual of manners? But before you put this reading down and go to the kitchen to dish out some ice cream, let's just go a teensy bit further into the business of manners (now that we've established that etiquette=manners, we can stop using that French term) and civility as they pertain to what you need to know and when. In particular, now is when you will realize you probably know nothing and therefore must watch and learn.

That reminds us, the first rule when learning manners is to learn when to watch and learn. If you find yourself in a dining situation where you don't know which fork to use or which bread plate is yours on the table, look for someone else who seems to be confident and follow their lead. In the end, even if it's incorrect; at least you're both using the wrong utensil. If this is the case, just be prepared to laugh at yourself if someone in the know decides to correct you both. No one will fault you if you retain a sense of humor when mistakes are made.

That said, in no particular order, we're going to list

some additional important standard operating procedures as they pertain to manners:

- Always take the high road and aim for professionalism. If you think something is questionable to do or wear you'll never regret being conservative rather than risk making a fool of yourself.

- Use common sense at all times. As mentioned earlier, if you don't know what to do about a question of etiquette (there's that French word again but sometimes it just sounds better, oui?) and don't have time to actually look up the answer (assuming it's one of those multiple choice things like 'should I do this or that?') then go with your gut. Presumably mom has already knocked some level of common sense into you by now, so make her proud and practice what you learned growing up. Unless, of course, you learned that eating with your fingers and burping at the table is acceptable. NOT.

- If you are uncertain as to what the dress code is wherever you are going, stay conservative. This is especially true if it's an event pertaining to work or a potential job. [Editor's Note: More on job related skills and acceptable protocol in Chapter 4]. Better to make your appearance with a polished, put-together look than to leave an impression of questionable decisions. ("She wore WHAT to the office party?"). Another rule of thumb is that you can always ask around to see what others will be wearing, but if that's not possible then make good choices. (Do we really need to remind you NOT to ask the guy that wears a bow tie with his plaid shorts and paisley shirt and still thinks it's a good look?)

- If you are asked to RSVP to an event or meeting, please be courteous and do so in a timely fashion. You're a grown up now. No excuses. The host would rather hear you can't come than have no response from you at all. On the other hand, if you respond that you can't attend, do not go into a lengthy explanation as to why you won't be there. Believe it or not, the most important thing is that you let the host know for purposes of a head count. He/she really does not care that your dog is sick or your ankle is swollen or whatever. Excuses are (almost) always lame and unacceptable to whomever the host is, so just accept that you can't go and let them know by the deadline they have requested. This is how civilized people deal with these things. Be one.

- <u>Don't over commit yourself, your time, and your resources</u>. If you think you can't do something then if the situation calls for it, briefly explain why you can't and walk forth in confidence that you made the right decision. Regrets are hard to live with.

- <u>As a follow up to the above, don't be a no-show</u>. Particularly when you have responded that you would attend.

- <u>Know how to introduce yourself and also how to introduce to others someone you've brought with you</u>. Basic guidelines being to raise your head and make eye contact when saying your name, speak clearly, and try to have one or two small things to say about yourself rather than just your name. If you bring someone, make sure to clarify whether they are a date, business associate or just plain friend. An example of this would be "I'd like you to meet my friend, Sara", or "this is my boss, Mr. Todd."

- <u>Communicate, communicate, communicate</u>. If it's by text, make sure you spell check; by phone, speak clearly and slowly; in writing, keep it professional, and it bears worth saying again, spell check. As a graduate, it is simply not acceptable to send any written communications with misspelled words and in sloppy form.  And if you think your tweets and emails are not subject to these rules you are just plain wrong.  In fact, the manner in which you communicate is almost as important as the act itself, so think twice before sending out a sloppy message, and never, ever copy people that don't need to be involved or hit "reply to all" unless (duh) they all need to see your response.  Just because the email was sent to a group does not mean that everyone is interested in all the responses, so think twice before sending.

- Speaking of texting, it should go without saying that most of what is texted is unnecessary gibberish and yet we all partake in some guilt of doing same.  If you really want to save humanity from extinction, how about going back to having face to face conversations with people on meaningful topics?    Developing this communication skill will be far more useful than using your thumbs to tap out another message about what you're having for dinner tonight.  Just sayin'.

- Learn how to use the phone.  Please.  It's the adult thing to do.  Long before there was texting and twitter and emails there were meaningful phone conversations.

- Contrary to what some say, (most) women appreciate it when a man opens a door or holds an elevator for them.  I hope that's not a shocking statement to you, but if it is so be it.  We've taken countless unofficial polls on this subject with females of all ages and it's unanimous – women do like to be treated special.  If you're a guy and have always wondered why women would enjoy this act of kindness just watch any James Bond movie and listen to the girls in the room swoon when he 'does his thing'.  It's called acting with finesse or confidence.    It's also called being kind and considerate; aka manners.  If you're rolling your eyes right now please stop. This is the real world speaking to you so take note if you want to play nice and get along with others.

- <u>Conversely, ladies, if you find yourself in a situation where a guy is doing the above you and it makes you uncomfortable, then you haven't quite finished your charm school lessons yet.</u> When it comes to manners, we must learn to both give and receive as the confidence issue gets more important as we age and seek better employment and more civility in the world. Practice your 'please' and 'thank yous' right along with your honest responses such as "Wow, that was really nice of you!" As mom no doubt told you, a little charm can go a long way.

- <u>Speaking of please and thank you, please use liberally</u>.

- <u>Same goes for sir, ma'am</u>. If the person you are addressing is older than you by all means feel free to address them with this level of respect, even if you were raised up North and believe this to be just a quaint Southern tradition, which it's not. This is also true when you are professionally addressing someone of title such as The President, an Ambassador or religious person. You may not agree with what their job stands for but showing respect for them having achieved it is expected when practicing civility.

- <u>When dining out in social or business affairs, please proceed with caution</u>. It wouldn't hurt to take a few minutes beforehand to familiarize yourself with a formal place setting and/or basic social skills; all things that can easily be Googled or viewed on a quick You Tube video. One of the most basic dining rules to remember about your place setting would be the BMW guide – Bread (separate smaller plate to the upper left side of your dinner plate), Meal (actual dinner plate), and Water/Wine/beverage (to the upper right of your dinner plate). Yes, it's that simple. Of course there are all kinds of varying degrees of this depending on how many courses are served and what utensils are on the table, but if you can only remember the BMW guide you've got a good start. Multiple utensils? Start with the fork or knife on the outside and work your way in with each new course. And as a refresher, what have we already learned about this situation? Don't be the first one to start eating! Instead, wait a few minutes and then follow the lead of the table host or someone who looks confident and polished.

- <u>The art of creating interesting conversation, whether at the dinner table or other social settings, is always appreciated</u>. Remember those awkward meals at home when no one had anything to say? It gets even worse as you grow older and are out in public. Everyone has something to say (remember all those ridiculous texts you keep sending?), so if this is a problem area for you do everyone a favor and bring at least one interesting topic to the table in case everyone else is speechless. Oh, and please talk responsibly.

- <u>Drink in moderation, please, PLEASE; drink in moderation</u>. Alcohol is potent and does not mix well with the following: job interviews, business appointments, family reunions, driving, texting, picture taking, participating in sporting events, giving toasts at weddings, introducing speakers, and well, the list is endless. But then you learned all that the hard way getting through school, right? In fact, just about the only thing we can think of that might be enhanced by drinking adult beverages would be dancing. Even then, dance responsibly. Please.

Okay, had enough? We realize this is just a starter kit for you when it comes to manners, but didn't we mention that much of it is also common sense?  Even if you've had no formal training, when it comes to the majority of us regular folks, common sense and politeness usually trumps all ceremonial rules.  Now, should you choose a formal profession, especially one in the military or Foreign Service, and then you might want to invest in some official instructions.  This is what is referred to as Protocol training, and there are excellent schools out there to assist you with this process.  I happen to be familiar with and hold several certificates of completion from the Global PEC Academy (Protocol, Etiquette and Civility)   -   www.globalpecacademy.com  - based in Dallas, TX, and there are others out there as well.

**"Being ignorant is not so much a shame as being unwilling to learn to do things the right way." [Benjamin Franklin]**

3

# GIFTS THAT GRADS
# NEED ALONG WITH
# SOME HELPFUL ADVICE

Every graduation season is a time when the stores fill up with all kinds of enticements for what kind of gifts to guy. Gadgets, goodies, and gimmicks – you can find one of everything that someone, somewhere will believe should be in the hands of the grad. As you may imagine, we have plenty of experience in this department, both the giving and receiving of these favors, so we can now tell you with certainty the gifts most likely to be filed in the 'nice idea but kind of lame' category, at least by our unofficial but popular polls:

**Nice Idea but Kind of Lame Gifts:**

- Ink pens, no matter how elegant. These days grads don't appreciate the sophistication of this instrument, nor do they write that much. And sadly, it will be quickly lost.

- Large books with lots of pages and words (too reminiscent of the expensive textbooks they just trashed. Ooops mom and dad. That might be a shocker but believe me it's most likely the truth.) NOTE: If your grad happens to be a voracious reader, and we sincerely hope they are, then by all means go ahead with this one. Just make sure it's a book that they have expressed interest in and not something like The Sam Walton Story Including Everything You Ever Wanted to Know about Wal Mart (if such a book exists). A better choice might be the Steve Jobs bio or How the Lady Found Her Ga-Ga (again, if such a book exists). We think you get the picture here, yes?

- Commemorative stuffed animals with mortar board hats for everyone to sign. Then what?

- Pots, pans, and miscellaneous household/kitchen items. Those gifts are wonderful for bridal showers and weddings, but just not cool for graduation. Besides, mom and dad haven't even had a chance to sort out all the boxes of tools and supplies that the grad has brought back with them from college. When they do get to that task, it will be full of surprises, meaning everything that you did NOT buy for your kid when you sent them off to school four years ago, and all kinds of things that you did NOT authorize your money to purchase. Spoiler Alert to the Parents: You can bank on finding a minimum of 25 different shot glasses, but where the items went that you did buy will forever remain an unsolved mystery.

- Photo albums or picture frames. We loved them in the past but it's a digital world now, so leave those challenges up to the individual to figure out how to file, categorize and label all those pictures they keep taking; and rest assured they are indeed taking as many if not more than we did with our Kodaks and Polaroids.

**Now, for the real deal. What the current grads want as told to us by well, current grads:**

- Cash and/or money of any denomination

- Gift certificates to places that they go (think popular restaurants, computer gadget stores, etc.,)

- Gift certificates to things that they use (ITunes, long distance phone cards if they are taking an overseas trip). For an accurate, up to date list of this category ask the parents what charges they see on those credit cards bills they're still paying on behalf of their son/daughter.

- A good leather portfolio or briefcase for holding resumes during job interviews

- Tickets to local attractions or movie theatres (hey, everyone needs a little fun in life, right?)

- Personalized 'promissory notes' wherein you pledge to take them out to an adult dinner at a fancy restaurant (HINT: this can also be a teaching-you-social-manners lesson in a fun way for both of you), or spend some time sharing a special talent you have like balancing the checkbook (or in new lingo that they'll understand, debit account reconciliation), public speaking skills, or anything else that they might otherwise be learning the hard way or not at all.

- Money that is specifically earmarked for something they must have such as a new suit for job interviews or maybe even those interview shoes that will soon be replacing the flip flops and tennies.

- Airline and hotel mileage points that can be gifted towards an upcoming trip

- A set of professional thank you cards, monogrammed, engraved, or plain (yes, it's time to put the Hello Kitty cards away)

Are we seeing a pattern of self-centeredness here? Welcome to the new generation of practical gift giving. This is also known as being realistic. Few among us have money to waste and everyone prefers that their gift be among the cool or most appreciated, so why not give them what they want? When in doubt, ask for ideas and whenever possible, go directly to the parent or the grad themselves. You will all be glad you did.

4

# MAKING AN IMPACT DURING YOUR JOB INTERVIEW

First of all, recent grads need to realize that interviews are mostly about two things:

First impressions

Work potential of the applicant

Since the work potential part is totally up to the individual and what they bring to the table as far as talent, drive, ethics, work history, etc., we're going to concentrate on the first impressions part. After all, this is a guidebook and we are trying to lend some advice and direction every step of the way for our newly minted graduates. Further, since job interviews are generally the first step after graduation, we felt it was of maximum importance to include some assistance in going through this process.

For starters, here is a list of things you'll need to make an exceptional impact when going on your first interviews:

- A good suit in one of the following colors:

    o Navy blue – says you can trust me
    o Black – says I have power/authority
    o Dark brown – says I'm an excellent communicator
    o Grey – says I'm attentive and can do a good job for you

- A decent pair of dress shoes (ladies, this means close toed shoes, even if you think your purple striped pedicure is the cutest ever)

- A professional looking resume – clean, crisp, concise

- Something to contain your resume such as a briefcase, portfolio, or appropriate file folder, and a pen with paper to make some notes

- A good self-introduction ( also referred to as your elevator speech)

- A solid handshake

- Confidence in yourself

If you're a researcher, you might be concerned that this list is much shorter than others you've seen. Your graduate may even have been given a lengthy one from a college counseling session that looks much different than this. As always, we're striving to simplify the process and therefore have cut to the chase. So, if you pay close attention to all of the above and the discussion that follows we feel confident that you will agree these are the fundamental basics of all successful interviews.

And by the way, just to clarify, our definition of successful is not contained to actually getting the job offer from the interview. We feel that a successful interview is one where the candidate has left a positive impact on the interviewer. Whether or not the actual job under discussion is offered at the end of said interview is not always the point. Crazy thinking? Not in the new world order. Many times just getting your foot in the door for an interview is the number one goal. Often there isn't even a job available at the time of the interview, and further if there is a job the candidate might even know before walking in that door they don't have a chance in China of getting it. In this day and age, we all now know the power of networking, and this generation is using every angle they can to get positioned for interviews with companies that aren't even hiring at the moment. But rest assured that one impressionable interview can lead to networking among executives and next thing you know there's another call from another company and another chance to get your name and resume out there. That's what aggressive, successful job candidates do these days, and by utilizing the above check list you will have already begun this process with a distinct advantage. So, let's get started.

The suit. The all-important first impression suit. Even if right now you are rolling your eyes thinking "I'm never going to work at a place that requires me to wear a suit every day!" whether you're male or female, at some point in your life you're going to need one, so why not get it now and put it to good use? It doesn't have to be expensive, it just has to be polished, and as mentioned above, in one of the dark or accepted colors. Interviewing in a bright orange dress, although trendy is not (universally) acceptable unless you are going for a job in the fashion industry, in which case you still have to use common sense and good judgment about your appearance. If you don't have the money to purchase a good suit then put this on your wish list for grad gifts and then be very thankful when those contributions come in. This one item could possibly pay you or your parents back tenfold for all those educational expenses you have endured over the years. The suit could even fall under the category of most useful item in your arsenal of getting you on the right track for professional employment. Yes, it's that important.

Now, we know many of you students – the ones we mentioned above that are rolling their eyes at the thought of having to wear a suit for a job interview – think they will be interviewing at really cool tech companies where people wear jeans and flip flops every day. Or better yet, conducting all interviews via their computer since the presumed job will be in cyberspace. Well guess what? You don't work there yet. You're still trying to get a foot in the door to get noticed and ultimately hired, so make every opportunity count. Dress responsibly.

And don't laugh but even the most expensive looking suit can be ruined if paired with the wrong shoes. It makes no sense to finish off your attempt at a professional look by wearing tennis shoes or fancy flip flops (and yes, it does happen, and yes, it doesn't make a good first impression. It's like you're half trying). We don't need to say too much more on this subject except to address the reason why so many students are now still shaking their heads and rolling their eyes at this discussion. Well, here's why:

Remember the phrase 'Making an Impact' in the title of this chapter? Well that's what we're aiming for here. If you can't make the effort to at least try for a favorable impression on your first job interviews, then when will you? Enough said.

Let's move on to the resumes. Presumably you've had some counseling while in school on the formatting of this document so we're not going to get into specifics on the set up. However, we need to speak to the overall appearance and presentation. Clean white paper, crisp lines with clear headings and easy to read details, along with the listing of only pertinent information. If you are applying for a job in the food industry and you won the taco eating contest at your college football weekend, you might want to save that tidbit for when the interviewer asks the question, "Tell me something interesting about yourself." Fascinating as it is (?), it doesn't belong in the body of the resume. If you're short on actual work experience then by all means add your volunteer projects, church and student groups or things that perhaps have enhanced your overall work ethic, but rarely do frivolous social activities augment your job capabilities. Having said that, there are always exceptions, but as with all the advice we are giving, use good judgment.

And please, for the love of all things professional, do not just carry your resume by itself into the interview. It belongs in something, anything that says "protect me in a professional way." Backpacks, most of them anyway, should not be used, mostly because they're too large and all beat up by the time you graduate. If yours looks half way decent and that's all you've got then make the best of it. Large purses are also not the best container, although if the resume is also in a file folder that you can quickly retrieve from your purse or backpack then that might be acceptable, though not ideal. The most professional presentation of your resume would be to have a leather portfolio or other business looking envelope or file container in your hands when entering the room. Remember, you need an open hand for that all important hand shake upon entering, so to carry a solid document case that contains your resume is not only a professional presentation but also gives you a prop of sorts to help with your potential nervousness. Placing this portfolio in your lap after you sit keeps your hands securely in place while hanging on to it and also allows for the presence of any additional paperwork you might have brought such as an accomplishment page listing awards/citations you may have earned, certifications, referral letters, a head shot, paper and pen for taking notes, etc.

What's that, you're asking? Why should I even have to take a resume when I've already filled out the on line application and attached my resume to that? Well, you are most certainly welcome to go in empty handed, but remember when we mentioned we're trying to help you make a good impact? Then listen up and take heed. The reality is that in the corporate world, many times the initial application enters through the human resources department but doesn't get passed on to the people actually doing the interview. So be like a Girl Scout and come prepared. What can it hurt?

**The final three bullets on the above list are possibly the deal breakers so listen up.** As a reminder, they are a good self-introduction, a solid handshake, and confidence in yourself. The first two can and should be practiced. The final one is acquired, and hopefully you got it when you walked across that stage and accepted your diploma in front of the cheering crowd.

We're not going to devote much time to the handshake other than to stress the importance of it. The best advice we can give on this topic is to make a commitment and stick with it. That's the correct mindset of a good handshake. Don't be a wimp and offer a limp hand or worse, finger or two. Find a grip and make it count. There should be solid contact, simultaneous movement with the recipient's hand, a slight squeeze and then release. What more can we say? It's not difficult, so don't screw it up. Oh, and don't forget to look the other person in the eye when making hand to hand contact. That's a reinforcement of the confidence factor. Looking away tells them you're uncomfortable. Eye to eye says you're ready for whatever conversation lies ahead. And finally, if you're the sweaty palms and bad breath type please wipe your hands first and don't forget the breath mints!

Now, the self- introduction part can be tricky.

Depending on whether or not you have already met the person you're interviewing with, you will have to gauge what you say about yourself. For purposes of this dialogue, let's assume it's your first time meeting the other person. It is really important to get the pronunciation of both your names correct at the start. Yes, both. You want to remember whoever is conducting this interview so you should repeat their name after they've spoken. "So nice to finally meet you, Mr. Punjab." If either name is a little challenging to articulate then this part is critical. You don't want to make a huge blunder by mispronouncing the name of your potential employer, and if they like and want to hire you there would definitely be a problem if they already thought you were someone else. Don't laugh, interviewers have told me that they start a day with a desk full of resumes and applications and many times get confused about which appointment is next! It can be awkward, but correct any mistakes at the outset and move on. Another sign of a person who has confidence? The ability to politely correct others without the need to apologize. Getting names right is really important so don't screw it up.

Moving on past the handshake with eye contact and repeating of the names (whew!), you may need to add something memorable once you've both sat down like "Thank you so much for meeting with me today, Mr. Andrews. As you may know, I just got back from my volunteer month building a school in Africa with my fraternity which is something I've always wanted to do, so I really appreciate you holding off on this interview until I could catch my breath." Of course, even something minor like "I saw your company's TV advertisement during the world series last night and was so excited to know that I'd be interviewing here today" can still be a good starting point for conversation and might give you a reason to be remembered. It could also provide further discussion points, in this example perhaps sports or even the advertisement itself, so never overlook that opportunity to make a quick connection with anything that could spark interest in you as an employee.

Beyond that, be prepared for saying something about yourself at an appropriate opportunity because it most definitely will come at some point during an interview. Even if the process seems like it's only covering boring, standard stuff, experience tells us that there is almost always an opening to talk about yourself and possibly to ask questions about the job or the company. Don't miss the chance to make this interview memorable and make sure you've given thought and preparation to what you will say or ask. Remember, you might think you've lead a mundane life but maybe all those science or writing awards you amassed during your youth could be interesting or relevant in some way to the job at hand. Or maybe not, but they could still get you remembered by the very fact that you pointed out one of your strengths that may not have been mentioned in your resume. And maybe, just maybe, even though the interviewer's title says "Chief Scientist', in putting yourself out there with something personal, you discover that the person doing the interview is also a gourmet home chef like you. How nice would that connection be?

So, we've given you the high lights of what we know for sure is important in order to make an impact during your interviews, and now we'd like to leave you with a few more tips:

- Smile. Breathe. Relax. Smile. Repeat.

- Remember your posture and body language is equally as important to the overall presentation. You can look great and slouch in a chair and you can bet you'll be remembered for slouching in the chair.

- If you have trouble remembering names try to use a

rhyme game as 'his name is Pete and isn't he neat' or make a word association like "Ms. Winters wore white."

• Always ask for a business card of whoever interviews you. If you also have one to give, make sure to present it correctly while holding the top corners with both hands and with your name on the card facing them.

• Make sure to follow up with appropriate thank yous to everyone that interviewed you. Always.

• At the conclusion of the interview, make sure you are clear on whatever lies ahead. This is your time to clarify what the next step in the hiring process will be such as inquiring about the timing of filling this position, who should you expect a call from and when, etc. Don't be shy. You want to make sure you don't leave until you know if you have a chance and when they will make a decision. Bring closure that you're comfortable with because you might not get another chance to ask any unresolved questions.

• Prior to the interview, if you are able to get yourself some business cards, please do. They can be done inexpensively on line or quickly at many print shops. Is should simply contain your contact information and possibly areas of specialty listed such as computer skills, college degree, graduated Cum Laude, or anything pertinent. Even a tag line as simple as "I want to be your next great employee!" can be a good reminder to them of how anxious you are to get the job. NOTE: If you haven't already done so, this would be a great time to drop the 'sexychic@hotmail.com' email address you've been using and get a professional one. Just do it.

- Make sure to turn off your cell phone as soon as you enter the building for the interview, and for the love of all things holy, please DO NOT attempt to answer any texts or phone calls during the course of this interview. Pretty please; we're begging you. We're fairly certain your BFF can wait another hour or so before you discuss what type of latte she had this morning. Right now it's kind of important that you focus on the job interview, okay?

- Smile. Breathe. Relax. Smile. Repeat.

Finally, do we even need to remind you at this point of the necessity of keeping your Facebook page, twitter account and anything else you maintain for social media in professional presentation mode? Yes, we do, don't we! There. That was your reminder. Don't make us say it again. We're already tired of hearing us say it, but apparently a lot of you just aren't listening. After graduation, no one – we repeat NO ONE – is interested in pictures of your beer chugging episodes and wild escapades during your school days. It may have been humorous and entertaining for you at the time, but this is now the real world where obtaining and keeping a job is paramount to advertising how many flavors of Vodka you have tasted in one night. Enough said? We hope so.

**"Don't mistake activity for achievement – practice it the right way." [John Wooden]**

# 5

# TRANSITIONING FROM STUDENT TO PROFESSIONAL

As you can imagine, there is a transition process connected with moving out of the college and dorm life into that of working full time in the real world. To some it will be shocking; to others, not so much. If you're in the latter group congratulations. You and your parents should be proud that you made it through phase one of life (schooling and education) and feel ready to move on to whatever lies ahead. You might not even feel the need to read the rest of this chapter, but since we've had your attention this far why not see it through until the end?

So this chapter is going to focus mostly on 'the rest of you'- the majority of grads who feel like they fumbled their way through the last four years and with or without an immediate job opportunity, still need some advice to transition back into reality, aka life after college. Below we've identified four main areas that you might want to think about as you carve the road ahead:

1) Get organized

2) Respect the clock

3) Prioritize

4) Work with mentors


We'll start with the <u>organization</u> part because t's easiest. First, get rid of all that junk you collected over the last four years – posters, beer pong cups, arts and craft items made from miscellaneous parts of beer cans and bottles, that puzzling and jumbled collection of silverware and other kitchen utensils you've amassed, socks and other layers of clothing that are not yours and you have no idea how they got in your drawers to begin with, etc., etc. You get the picture here. We realize they all hold memories for you (well, maybe not the socks), but carrying such items over in the next phase of your life is like carrying excess baggage. Better to clean things out now, especially before mom and dad have to rent a truck to haul it all home and then rent a storage unit in which to keep your precious but useless items. Taking the time to clean things out now is healthy and freeing. If you're moving to another city you will most likely want to start clean with your decorating and apartment set ups, so don't haul all that old junk around with you. Consider this a fresh start on every aspect of your life and take the time to sort through everything. And while you're doing it make sure to recycle things that are still usable to someone, somewhere. The golden rule about one man's junk is another's treasure is never truer than when college kids are cleaning out their stash. Some things may be useful to an incoming freshman; others will have to go to Good Will or even the garbage. If this is too painful for you to do alone rest assured your parents will love to assist going through all these belongings to see exactly where their money has been spent over the last few years. And, if that thought doesn't get you quickly moving through the task at hand nothing will!

Respecting the clock could be the biggest adjustment of all for you. We sincerely hope not, but if you're anything like most of the grads we know you're used to living and functioning on whatever time zone you've set for yourself over the last few years; and many times that 'system', or should we say lack thereof (?), will no longer work for you. Unless you are fortunate enough to be self-employed, once you get a job there will be timelines, lots of them. And, most companies don't have a high tolerance level for any of the following: being late for work, missing scheduled meetings, leaving work earlier than allowed, neglecting project deadlines, taking long lunches and breaks as well as generally ignoring any structured activity within the confines of what was outlined in the job before you accepted it. So like it or not, you are now on a 24/7 time card. If your cell phone service is unreliable, get a watch to keep track of time. No excuses. Get used to it and make the necessary adjustments as quickly as you can. And helicopter parents be forewarned: if you think you're doing junior a favor by providing a personal wake-up call every morning so they can get to work on time you're living in a fantasy world.

Prioritization. This really shouldn't be too difficult once you get a job and place to stay. After those things are determined, your priorities – eat, work, sleep, repeat – may fall easily into place. The hard part will be to find some of that precious personal time you used to have so much of, but trust us, you will find some. It might not be as much as you want but that's why it's so important to identify exactly what your priorities are from the start. If you can't miss Grey's Anatomy on Thursday night or have to run your 5K every Saturday morning then make sure those activities are plugged into your schedule. Twenty four hours a day, seven days a week. That's what we all have to work with. Get used to it and make your time count. And please respect the time of others as much as you do your own. If you're scheduled for a meeting or even a cup of coffee with your friends, don't make them wait unnecessarily or be a no show.

The final area, <u>working with mentors</u>, is one we sincerely hope you develop and use wisely. For many of you, this will be an extension of a process that you started during school. Maybe there were some teachers or counselors you came to depend on for help and assistance? Well, no matter what your circumstances after graduation, you will still benefit from reaching out to others for support along this journey. Your mentors may change from time to time depending on your needs, but by all means don't be afraid to ask for support and guidance whether your needs are work related or personal. Make friends with your bankers (we realize this could be a shocking experience for some as many of you think your banker is actually an automated ATM machine, but you do know there are real people inside that facility, right?), find a mentor in another department at your work, talk to your older siblings and/or dare we suggest your parents? Older and wiser people love to give advice, in fact, that's what this whole book is about. The 'been there done that and now we want to share' premise, and we truly hope you're learning as you read along.

And speaking of advice, in our final chapter we're leaving you with a collection of ideas we've found useful and hope that you do, too. So don't leave us now – please read on!

"You know, I sincerely hope you enjoy this next chapter of your life because it's really going to be great, as long as you pay your taxes. And don't just take a year off because you think Uncle Sam is snoozing at the wheel because he will descend upon you like a hawk from hell. Let's just put it this way. After some past indiscretions with the IRS, my take home pay last year was $9,000.00." [Will Ferrell in his Class Day speech to Harvard Students, 2003]

# 6

# PUTTING IT
# ALL TOGETHER

### Top Ten Pieces of Advice for Graduates:

1) Volunteer for everything you can, both at work and leisure time, while you're still young and single (and also afterward, but it gets more challenging then). It's all a learning experience and also looks good on your resume.

2) Learn how to take criticism without having your feelings hurt, and also how to give it constructively. This is a critical concept in the work force.

3) Figure out a budget and live within it. Make sure it's realistic and not based on that dream job and salary that may or may not happen for you. Ask your parents how expensive life is.

4) Communication is a two way street. Don't just listen to others. Even if it's uncomfortable for you, engage yourself in conversation. The more you do it the more natural it will seem. Everyone should have something to contribute to the ongoing dialogues in life.

5) Take every opportunity to work on your public

presentation skills by speaking up in office meetings, volunteer groups, and other activities. This will strengthen your leadership capabilities, and the more you do it the more confident you will become. Plus good orators usually get better jobs!

6) Read. Read. Read. Everything you can get your hands on. That's how you learn more about the world around you, and it makes for more interesting interchanges among friends and associates.

7) Listen. Shhh. Sometimes you can learn from the silence.

8) Practice things that occur repeatedly in your life like introducing yourself (think about how you want the other person to remember you) and answering that all important command, "tell me a little bit about you." It will come up repeatedly in your life so better to be prepared with an answer, preferably a better one than "well, there's not really much to tell."

9) Always be ready to network by asking for an exchange of contact information when appropriate. Either via your smart phone data entry and/or carrying your own business cards

10) Understand and accept that your first job is most likely not your dream job. That's why you should never stop dreaming.

BONUS TIP: Call home, and do it often. You will be missed!

**"Our world is a college, events are teachers, happiness is the graduating point, character is the diploma God gives man." [Newell Dwight Hillis]**

# BONUS READING

# AUTHOR'S ADDITIONAL
# FIVE CENTS WORTH

As promised earlier in this book, there follows something I penned and gave to my own kids when they graduated. I hope this is food for thought about what you should now say to your own grad, so after reading this, feel free to take author's liberty by putting pen to paper and writing your own version to share.

**TEN THINGS I WISH MY PARENTS HAD TOLD ME WHEN I WAS YOUR AGE** (lovingly compiled by your mom):

1) <u>How much my father was earning and how much life cost</u>. Because I came from a family that didn't really discuss money issues or the potential lack thereof (if we bought 'fill in the blank'), it never occurred to me how expensive that item was in relation to whatever my dad was making at the time. Somehow they always provided without complaining (much). Therefore, the reality of finding a job that would provide enough money to live in the lifestyle to which I was already accustomed (and then some) and working at it for the rest of my life was rather shocking. So, chose jobs

wisely and remember this about money: It doesn't buy happiness; it buys options which make happiness more likely.

2)  That long term goals are far more important than short term ones. If a decision is hard to make it must be because it's important to you or someone else, or possibly both. Think long and hard about life-changing issues like marriage, kids, job offers, and stock options, but make quick decision about what movie to see or restaurant you want on Saturday night. As they say, don't sweat the small stuff.

3)  That communication, at every level, is the key to successful survival. Converse with your family. Have meaningful conversations with friends. If you're having a bad day, tell your mom/dad and tell them why. As parents, we can't read your mind, especially if you're living away from us. Maybe, just maybe we could even help. And when you're having a good day, thank BOTH your parents and your God. Remember that communication includes talking, greeting people you meet, reading, writing and a whole bunch of other things, too. Most problems of all levels arise because someone has not communicated their feelings or problems in a timely fashion to enlist help or guidance.

4)  That my first apartment would not come equipped with main service, a laundry lady, chef, clean sheets, a personal organizer to handle my scheduling needs, accountant, chauffeur to run my errands, decorator, a wallet full of money to draw from when I didn't feel like cooking myself dinner and a loving family to greet me morning, noon and night. Little did I know it would be pitiful in decoration, lacking in space, always void of food, and cost more than I could afford on my first salary. It also came with plugged toilets, dirty dishes and floors, dust everywhere, and no one else living in it to fix these problems or clean for me!

Remember the words of Louise May Alcott: I am not afraid of storms for I am learning how to sail my ship.

5) <u>That security in my surroundings is of utmost importance to my happiness</u>. Doors and windows that lock. Lighting that is sufficient and always works. A safe place to park my car. Neighbors who are good and kind people. Direct deposit of my paycheck. Enough money to buy adequate insurance and still contribute to my savings plan. A balanced checking account that always has at least enough money in it so that I can withdraw money when necessary without embarrassing or frustrating problems. Security comes in many different forms.

6) <u>How to manage my money</u>. There is no better way to get rich and feel good about yourself than to understand how to manage your hard earned wages. This includes living on a budget, living within said budget, planning for the future, making investments and saying 'no' when you can't afford something.

7) <u>That I should ask people questions – lots of them – especially about themselves or things that they know and I need to know</u>. If you ask people about themselves you will be fascinating to them. If you ask them to explain something, they will be proud to share their expertise. If you don't know something you must ask about it or risk looking like a fool or making mistakes. All you have to do is ask.

8) <u>That when you pick your life partner, even if you stay married to the same person until the end, that person will very likely be a completely different person by the time you both check out.</u>

9) <u>If you get in a rut, don't decorate it</u>. Get out of it! And don't hold anyone but yourself accountable for it.

10) <u>That on every mother's day, father's day, birthday and important event day of those people that I love the most I acknowledge that person in some special way</u>. Cards, phone calls, flowers, kind gestures and acknowledgment of any kind – it doesn't matter what you do it's that you remember to do it! Always remember that life is temporary and for any one of us each new day could be our last.

## WHAT WE ABSOLUTELY POSITIVELY
## KNOW FOR SURE

You can never offend anyone with kindness

Never underestimate the art of good conversation

Take every opportunity to stay in touch with family and friends

Hate is a four letter word that requires lots of energy

Love is a four letter word that requires lots of energy

Everybody loves to get personal mail, even if it's electronic

Never miss family reunion events. Every year people in your extended family will die.

Put names and dates on photos right away so you remember the details

No one ever regrets practicing safe sex

Call home – even/especially when you don't need a thing

Daily vitamins really do make a difference in your health

Child rearing is harder than childbirth

Good manners begin with good self-perception and confidence in your actions

Always stand tall. Good posture keeps you healthy and makes a better presentation

Know what your-self package is, in other words, how you present yourself to the world.

# ABOUT THE AUTHOR

As a writer, Terry likes to tell stories about people and places while sharing life experiences, and hopefully, readers will continue to enjoy them. She is both a published author and veteran meeting planner, the latter being a career which is pretty much summed up as 'making organization out of chaos.' Terry's success in both areas can be attributed, in part, to her motto which is "always sweat the small stuff." Her resume covers a wide range of international planning, management positions in hotels and major theme parks, speaking engagements about business issues, as well as motherhood and caring for "It's NOT my dog!" She maintains a blog called Hospitality Hive that can be found at www.hypeorlando.com/hospitality-hive and has an author's website with lots of good stories at www.tmlwrites.com. Tried and True is her first book, and its' purpose was to simplify a whole lifetime of on-the-job training into some easy to comprehend road rules for young business professionals and entrepreneurs as they enter a new work force that still requires a basic understanding of civility. PS – If the word 'civility' befuddles you, please read this book!